READER BONUS!

Dear Reader,

As a thank you for your support, Lynda Sunshine West would like to offer you a special reader bonus: a one-on-one coaching call to help you break through one fear today. During this 30-minute session, you will share one fear you want to break through and Lynda Sunshine will guide you on the steps you need to take to walk through that door of opportunity and get the result you're looking for.

This one-on-one coaching session typically **retails at $500 USD**, but as a valued reader, you are granted a one-time access at no cost to you. To claim your Fear Busting Session, simply follow this link http://fearbustersession.com and sign up today.

READER BONUS!

http://fearbustersession.com

DO IT
BECAUSE
YOU'RE SCARED

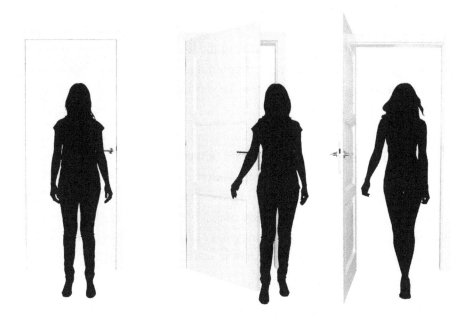

Opening Doors to Conquer Fear and
EMBRACE UNFORESEEN OPPORTUNITIES

Email: lynda@actiontakerspublishing.com

Website: www.actiontakerspublishing.com

ISBN # (paperback) 978-1-956665-36-9

ISBN # (Kindle) 978-1-956665-37-6

Published by Action Takers Publishing™

Table of Contents

Staying Connected

I'd love to hear from you. What fears have you had that you've confronted and kicked to the curb? What fears are you still working on? What fears have you not yet addressed?

I love receiving emails from people telling me how they've confronted their fears, so send an email to me at Lynda@ActionTakersPublishing.com.

I look forward to hearing from you.

Lynda Sunshine West
Founder & CEO
Action Takers Publishing

Introduction

When I was five years old, I ran away from home and was gone for an entire week. I only went to the next door neighbor's, but for all intents and purposes I was going to be gone forever. I'm sure the neighbor called my mom and told her I was there, but she let me stay. I thought my parents would come get me in a day, but one day turned into seven before my mom called the neighbor and told her it was time for me to come home, "Lynda's been gone long enough. You can send her home now." I'm pretty sure my mom was just trying to teach me a lesson, but that week became instrumental in my belief system. Nobody came to get me and I was instilled with a firm belief that no one wanted me around and nobody loved me. At five years old, this belief was locked in tight and I would believe that for the next 46 years, until I was 51 years old.

When I came home, I came home with my tail between my legs and my head bent down, literally. As you might imagine, I was growing up in an abusive home. I was afraid to look my parents in the eyes, and I wouldn't look at people in the eyes for decades. I was riddled with fear and, as a result, became a people-pleaser. Whenever people asked me to do anything, I would say "YES" because I was afraid that they wouldn't like me if I said "NO."

High school became a petri dish for fear. While I was saying yes to my friends, I was also lashing out at other students. Oh, man. If I could only turn back time. I would never have made fun of that girl. If I could remember her name, I would fall to my knees and beg for her forgiveness. My efforts to please one group caused me to be mean to others. Even my friends would make fun of me. To compensate, I started making fun of myself. The mean girl … became mean to herself.

This behavior of being mean to myself and allowing others to be mean to me didn't get any better after high school.

Right out of high school, I married someone just like my dad. I didn't recognize it as an abusive relationship because it was just a continuation of how I had grown up. My first husband yelled at me on a daily basis, "You're so stupid. You're so ignorant. People only like you because they feel sorry for you." And I believed him.

I ended the marriage after two years and two babies. It's incredible what emotional and mental damage can happen in just two years. I just decided one day that I'm not going to stay in an abusive relationship like my mom did, so I walked out the door with a diaper bag over one shoulder, my purse over the other, one child on my hip, and one child in her baby carrying case. That may sound like a brave thing to do, but I did it because my fear of staying was stronger than my fear of leaving.

My professional life had its own set of issues. I moved from job to job to job, a bank teller, data entry clerk at Fortune 500 companies, legal secretary for a judge in the Ninth Circuit Court of Appeals. Any of them could have been a long-term career, but I usually left anywhere from one week to 18 months of being hired. In other cases, I was underappreciated. I came up with new ideas and no one would listen. I was also afraid of saying the wrong thing and people thinking I was stupid. But whenever I did something "right," people called me a brown-noser.

So I started to shut down. I stopped using my voice. Was it because I was stupid like my ex-husband said I was? Could he have been right?

I was caught in this cycle where I felt afraid of failing, but I also felt afraid of succeeding. I couldn't find satisfaction in any of my 49 jobs.

It was August of 2014 when I was driving to work one day working for the judge in the Ninth Circuit Court of Appeals, my 49th job after 36 years in the corporate world, sitting in traffic like I had been doing for many decades. As I was sitting in that traffic, an overwhelming sense of dread and disgust and anger engulfed my body. Here I was, 51 years old, and I remember pounding on the steering wheel and saying "What is this all about, what is this planet all about, why are we here, why do we have to do this, what is my life all about, why am I here?"

That day when I got to work there was a post in a Facebook group that said "I'm a life coach. I took some time off and I'm getting back into it. I'm looking for five women who want to change their life." She was talking to me. I sent her a private message, said I wanted to work with her, and we worked together for the next five months.

The most instrumental exercise we did together helped me see myself through the eyes of others (positive people only), which, in turn, helped me transform from my own worst enemy into my own best cheerleader.

The amount of change that happened in that period of time was astronomical. People were saying to me on a weekly basis "You're so different this week than you were last week."

When December rolled around, I was on my own, all alone, no more help. I had the tools that she had supplied me with to keep growing, but I knew deep down that there was a LOT more growth to come. And I wanted it NOW!

At the end of December, I realized I had gotten so accustomed to changing and growing that I had become addicted to the positivity in my life. That positivity had slowed down because my life coach was no longer with me.

New Year's Eve isn't a big deal for me. My husband and I go to bed early and skip all the festivities. However, when I woke up on January 1, 2015, something was different. I realized I had so many fears that were stopping me from living my life. Rather than setting a New Year's Resolution (because I break them every time), I made a New Year's Commitment to break through one fear every day that year.

Every morning for 365 days I would wake up, before getting out of bed, and ask myself one simple question, three simple words that would change the trajectory of my life. Then I would wait for the answer to come. The question was "What scares me?"

The first three months I faced fears such as talking to strangers, starting a conversation, and going to networking events. I was feeling cautiously optimistic, but fear was still prominent.

About three months into facing one fear every day, I was brushing my teeth and reciting an acronym I had heard many times: False Evidence Appearing Real. False Evidence Appearing Real. False Evidence Appearing Real. Staring at myself, I realized that acronym is a lie.

I broke it down and realized that there was nothing false about my fear. My fears are as real as can be to me. There was no evidence in anything. It didn't appear real; it was real.

I looked over the previous three months and had this epiphany that when I tapped into my faith, it was much easier for me to break through my fear. You can't have faith and fear at the same time. They are opposites. I also realized that fear is nothing more than anxiety or nervousness so I came up with my own acronym:

Faith Erases Anxious Reactions

When your faith is strong, your fear is weak. You just need to tap into your faith (faith in yourself, faith in others, and faith in God).

I continued the process. Wake up, ask the question, wait for the answer, face the fear THAT DAY.

Over the next 90 days, I conquered fears such as asking someone to do something for me, speaking on stage, asking a celebrity to endorse my book.

After 180 days of fears, I looked back on the previous six months and asked myself a question, "What's the common theme between these fears? There's gotta be something." That's when I had another epiphany - the majority of my fears were based on the fear of judgment.

Something as simple as starting a conversation with a stranger can be difficult for many of us. In my case, it was the fear of saying something stupid or ignorant. For others, it may due to their speaking with an accent or not being an expert on a certain topic.

Armed with this knowledge, I was able to tackle the next six months with a mission to rid myself of the fear of judgment. By the end of the year, judgment was no longer an issue for me. I did it.

While I was ridding myself of the fear of judgment, I came up with a simple 7-step process to help me quickly and easily break through fear EVERY TIME.

The first thing you need to do is identify a fear you want to overcome. Maybe you're a rockstar at work… you know you're underpaid, but you're afraid of asking for a raise; maybe you have a great idea or passion to start a new business but the idea of starting it paralyzes you; maybe you're comfortable around friends, but meeting new people scares you; maybe you're comfortable speaking to small groups of people you know, but the idea of getting on an actual stage scares you. I have experienced ALL of these in the past, and, yes, they're all connected to the fear of judgment.

To demonstrate my simple 7-step process, let's use speaking on stage as the fear we're going to tackle today. This was actually my greatest fear, the one where my knees were shaking, my throat locked up, my palms were sweaty, and my memory escaped me once I got on stage.

They say more people are scared of speaking on stage than they are of dying. That is false. The truth is that more people are scared of the judgment they will receive while speaking on stage.

After you've identified your fear (I'm using the fear of speaking on stage in this example), the first question you ask yourself is … "If I [speak on stage] right now, will it adversely affect my life one year from today?"

Let's examine this sentence. The first component is to clearly state your fear.

Then we come to the phrase "right now." What's happening by asking this question is you are starting to move your brain into a state of logic and moving yourself out of an emotional state of mind.

You see, fear starts in the part of the brain called the amygdala. According to Smithsonian Magazine, "A threat stimulus, such as the sight of a predator, triggers a fear response in the amygdala, which activates areas involved in preparation for motor functions involved in fight or flight." That feeling of fighting or having to run away is a very visceral, emotional reaction that we can feel in our bodies. What we need to do to overcome fear is to start thinking logically.

Then we add the word "Adversely." Why that word? If you leave out the word "adversely," you're left with "will it affect my life." Yes, it can affect your life in a positive or negative way. By adding the word "adversely," you're asking yourself if doing this action will affect your life in a bad way.

Then we have the words, "One year." I start here because the majority of fears will not adversely affect your life one year from today. In the case of speaking on stage, the worst thing that may happen is you forget part of your talk and the audience is confused about the point you were trying to make. But a year from now, you may not even remember that day occurred. Time has a way of putting things into perspective. Seeing a situation with this timeframe puts you into a realistic state of mind and that is necessary in order to quickly and easily break through fears.

Finally, we have the words "from today." I was breaking through one fear every single day for a year, so it was important that I break through that fear that day. Waiting until tomorrow I would then have two fears to break through. This ended up being a brilliant idea because it forced me to exercise my fear breaking muscle. Breaking through fears became easier and easier because fear became part of my comfort zone. I ENLARGED the size of my comfort zone by doing this practice.

The second step is asking the same full question, but this time changing only the timeframe.

One Year changes to Six Months.

If I speak on stage right now and I mess up, will it adversely affect my life six months from today? Like the one-year timeframe, there is still no downside.

Then Six Months changes to One Month.

If I speak on stage right now and I mess up, will it adversely affect my life one month from today? Again, no downside, but we are getting closer to the present.

One Month changes to One Week.

If I speak on stage right now and I mess up, will it adversely affect my life one week from today? Here's where it gets a little funky. Depending on the fear you're facing, one week from breaking through the fear you may still feel a little queasy inside or weird. You may still feel the effects of breaking through that fear. This is because you've moved back into an emotional state of mind, even though, logically, you know you're okay. Let's say, for all intents and purposes, you responded that speaking on stage right now will NOT adversely affect your life one week from today.

As you might have guessed, the next steps are to shorten the timeframe.

<u>One Week</u> changes to <u>One Day</u>.

If I speak on stage right now and I mess up, will it adversely affect my life one day from today?

Let's go for even shorter.

<u>One Day</u> changes to <u>One Hour</u>.

If I speak on stage right now and I mess up, will it adversely affect my life one hour from today?

And FINALLY….

If I speak on stage right now and I mess up, will it adversely affect my life RIGHT NOW?

You might be wondering why I use seven steps instead of just one. Well, I found that by slowly stepping myself down through each time period, it moved me into a more relaxed state of mind and my logical brain had time to process what I was doing. I was able to more logically answer the questions and not allow my emotions take over logic and reality.

But what if the answer to the question is YES?

What I have found is that after you break through a fear RIGHT NOW, you rarely have long-term adverse effects. In those cases where an adverse outcome is "possible," you need to come up with a plan of how to address that. You don't just give up and walk away; you simply recognize that additional work needs to be done to overcome that fear.

If you're afraid of asking for a raise, your plan may be to rehearse what you are going to say to your boss and have an outline of WHY you deserve the raise.

If you're afraid of starting a new business, you may find a mentor who is successfully doing what you want to do and have them guide you so you gain confidence in starting your business.

If you're afraid of speaking on stage, you may rehearse your talk before getting on the stage.

If you're afraid of meeting new people, your plan may be to psyche yourself up before talking to them. I use a word that moves me into a state of confidence and laughter, which also calms my nerves. My word is "SHAZAM!!" What will be your word?

I may not have the same fears as you, but our fears are very real … to each of us. Let's decide right here right now not to allow anyone to rob us of our experience of that fear by telling us it's insignificant or ridiculous.

YOU have the power to break through that fear in that moment, but only you can make that decision. And it has to be a decision that you made FOR YOU.

Yes, fear is scary. But it doesn't have to control your life. In fact, it can make your life better. So when you've identified a fear in your life, face it head on and do it BECAUSE you're scared.

You never know who you won't meet until you step
through to the other side of that door.
~Lynda Sunshine West

· · · · · · · · ● ● ● ● ● ● ● ● ● · · · · · · · ·

CHAPTER 1

Fear Unleashed: Reclaiming Control Over Your Success

I don't know about you, but I like to dive right in. Are you open to that? If so, let's go.

In this chapter, we are going to delve into the gripping tale of Lynda Sunshine West's (that's me) personal journey, exploring the profound impact of fear on my life and the pivotal moment that sparked a transformative shift. With an authentic and captivating narrative, I will take you back to my childhood, where I ran away from home at the tender age of five and was gone an entire week, unknowingly setting the stage for a deeply ingrained belief that I was unwanted and unloved. This belief would continue to shape my decisions and overshadow my pursuit of success for the next 46 years.

You will witness the profound influence fear can exert over our lives, driving us to become people-pleasers, fearing judgment and rejection at every turn. My experiences in high school and beyond serve as poignant reminders of the detrimental effects of fear, leading to misguided actions and self-deprecation. Can you relate?

With vulnerability and introspection, I recount my abusive childhood and first marriage and my courageous decision to break free, illustrating the immense emotional and mental damage that can transpire within just a few short years. These experiences highlight the pervasive nature of fear and its ability to hold us captive, hindering personal growth and fulfillment.

Through my professional endeavors (I had 49 jobs in 36 years), I share how fear manifested itself in my career choices, from job-hopping to feeling underappreciated and stifled. The fear of failure and the fear of success became inextricably intertwined, creating a paradoxical struggle that left me yearning for true satisfaction and never finding it in a corporate job.

However, she experienced a profound moment of introspection during a traffic jam that served as a catalyst for change. Frustrated with the monotony of life and questioning its purpose, I stumbled upon an opportunity that would lead me down the path of transformation. A door of opportunity showed itself and I walked right through it not knowing the results that would come from that bold move. Engaging the services of a life coach, I embarked on a five-month journey that brought about remarkable changes and laid the foundation for a renewed perspective. That was the GREATEST gift I have ever given to myself, the gift of hiring someone to help me figure out who I am and what my purpose is for being on this planet. I was 51 years old and I'm so glad I raised my hand that day and hired Liz.

"See the opportunity, then seize the opportunity."
~Lynda Sunshine West

I truly believe that every single one of us has a purpose and once we figure out our purpose, it's our job and duty to live the rest of our lives on purpose rather than on accident. I believe this so much, that you can find a copy of our collaboration book, *"Finding Your Purpose: Living Live "On Purpose" Rather Than On Accident,"* on our website at www.ActionTakersPublishing.com.

This chapter sets the stage for a profound exploration of fear, its grip on our lives, and the possibility of reclaiming control over our own success. I'm hopeful that my journey serves as an inspiration, showcasing the power of self-reflection and the capacity to challenge long-held beliefs.

Let's get started.

Understanding Fear: Unmasking Its Grip on Achievement

If you've ever seen the Wizard of Oz, you probably remember the Cowardly Lion. He was scared of his own shadow. What makes us humans (and I guess lions) scared of our own shadows? Well, fear is a formidable force that can hold us back from reaching our full potential and hinder our pursuit of success. By unmasking its grip on achievement, we can begin to dismantle its power and reclaim control over our own destinies.

The greatest fear is the fear of judgment and often arises from a place of self-doubt and insecurity. By looking closely at self-doubt and insecurity, we can see that judgment is the underlying fear.

Self-doubt: It's a common human experience, and many people struggle with it at various points in their lives. Recognizing the underlying causes of self-doubt is the first step toward addressing and overcoming it. With self-awareness, supportive relationships, and a proactive mindset, we can gradually build self-confidence and challenge the self-doubt that holds us back from reaching our full potential.

Insecurity: Insecurity refers to a deep sense of self-doubt, inadequacy, or uncertainty about oneself and one's abilities. It's characterized by a lack of confidence and a constant fear of judgment or rejection. Insecurity often manifests in various aspects of life, including relationships, work, and personal achievements.

Individuals experiencing insecurity may harbor a persistent belief that they are not good enough or that others perceive them negatively. They may constantly compare themselves to others, seeking validation and reassurance to alleviate their doubts. Insecurity can be accompanied by feelings of anxiety, self-consciousness, and a heightened sensitivity to criticism.

It's essential to differentiate between occasional feelings of insecurity, which are common and experienced by most individuals at some point, and chronic insecurity which significantly hinders daily life. Chronic insecurity may require focused attention and support to address underlying issues and foster self-confidence. That's where my life coach (Liz) came in. Boy, I was insecure about so many things in my life. Had it not been for Liz, I have no idea where I'd be today (maybe on job #86).

Overcoming insecurity and any other fear involves developing self-awareness, challenging negative beliefs, and cultivating self-compassion. It requires recognizing and valuing one's strengths and accomplishments, embracing vulnerability, and working towards personal growth and self-acceptance. Finding someone to help is the first step. Just like you see in others what they don't see in themselves, others see in you what you don't see in yourself.

Like an invisible barrier, fear stands between us and our aspirations, whispering insidious doubts and convincing us to stay within the confines of our comfort zones (which isn't always all that comfortable). It's fueled by our past experiences, traumatic events, and the limiting beliefs we have internalized over time.

Moreover, fear can manifest in different forms. It can be paralyzing, preventing us from taking risks or pursuing opportunities. It can also be disguised as perfectionism, urging us to endlessly seek validation or avoid any possibility of criticism (again, fear of judgment). Fear thrives on uncertainty, exploiting our fear of the unknown and the potential pitfalls that may lie ahead.

By recognizing and acknowledging the presence of fear in our lives, we gain the power to challenge its dominance. This requires a willingness to confront our deepest fears head-on and delve into the discomfort that accompanies such introspection. It involves peeling back the layers of conditioning and self-limiting beliefs to uncover the truth about our own capabilities.

Through my own journey, I have come to understand the profound impact of fear on my life. It held me captive for many years, dictating my choices and perpetuating a cycle of self-doubt. At age 51, I refused to let fear define me any longer. You don't have to wait that long.

I invite you to join me in this exploration of fear, to examine your own fears and trace their origins. Let us together confront the discomfort and confront the limiting beliefs that have held us back. By shedding light on fear's hold over our achievements, we can begin to dismantle its power and open ourselves up to a world of possibilities.

Imagine what your life will be like when you are able to look fear in the face and say, "Ahhhh, that's just fear. I'm going to do it BECAUSE I'm scared."

> *"You'll never know who you won't meet until you step outside of your comfort zones."* Lynda Sunshine West

The Psychology of Fear: How It Shapes Our Thoughts and Actions

Fear is not merely a fleeting emotion; it has a profound impact on our psychology and influences the way we think, perceive, and act in the world. At its core, fear is a survival mechanism deeply rooted in our evolutionary history. It activates the amygdala, a part of our brain responsible for processing emotions and triggering the fight, flight, or freeze response. This primal response is designed to protect us from imminent danger and ensure our physical survival. When faced with a genuine threat, such as encountering a predator in the wild, fear mobilizes our body's resources, heightens our senses, and prepares us for swift action.

In today's modern world, though, many of the fears we experience aren't immediate physical threats. They are often psychological and emotional in nature, rooted in our perception of potential harm or negative outcomes. These fears can be equally powerful, hijacking our cognitive processes and influencing our thoughts and behaviors.

When I ran away at five years old, it was my fear of my dad that helped me make that decision to run away. I "moved" to a safe environment (my neighbor's house). I didn't feel safe at the house I grew up in, so I made a change of venue. I did something about it.

But, when I came home after a week (my mom called the neighbor and told her, "It's time to send Lynda home now"), I became riddled with fears and became a people-pleaser. Moving from a place of safety to a place of fear created a barrier around me that would prevent me from branching out of my own little cocoon for many decades. One way fear shaped my thoughts was by narrowing my focus and attention.

When fear arises, our attention becomes fixated on the perceived threat, creating a cognitive tunnel vision. This tunnel vision narrows our perspective, making it difficult to see alternative possibilities or solutions. We become preoccupied with the potential negative outcomes, which can limit our creativity, problem-solving abilities, and overall decision-making process.

Fear also has a significant impact on our beliefs and self-perception. When we experience fear repeatedly or intensely, it can erode our self-confidence and instill a sense of self-doubt. We may develop negative beliefs about our capabilities, worthiness, or deservingness of success. These self-limiting beliefs can further perpetuate fear, creating a vicious cycle of avoidance and self-sabotage.

Fear influences our behavior and choices. It can lead us to adopt risk-averse tendencies, as we instinctively try to protect ourselves from potential harm. Fear can hold us back from taking necessary risks, pursuing opportunities, or stepping outside of our comfort zones. It restricts our personal growth and limits our potential for fulfillment and achievement.

Understanding the psychology of fear is crucial for reclaiming control over our thoughts and actions. By gaining insight into the underlying mechanisms of fear, we can develop strategies to navigate it more effectively. It starts with cultivating self-awareness, recognizing our own fears, and understanding how they influence our thoughts and behaviors.

Through this awareness, we can begin to challenge our automatic fear responses and shift our mindset. We can engage in practices that promote self-compassion, allowing ourselves to acknowledge our fears without judgment. This self-compassion creates a supportive inner environment that fosters courage and resilience in the face of fear.

Empowering Mindset Shift: Overcoming Fear's Influence on Success

Let's explore the empowering mindset shift that is necessary to overcome the pervasive influence of fear on our path to success. Fear has a remarkable ability to hold us back, but by cultivating the right mindset, we can break free from its limitations and unlock our true potential.

The first crucial aspect of this empowering mindset shift is acknowledging that fear is a natural and universal human experience. It's important to recognize that fear is not a sign of weakness or incompetence; It's an inherent part of being human. By normalizing fear and understanding that everyone encounters it at various points in their lives, we remove the stigma and shame often associated with it.

This realization empowers us to face our fears head-on, knowing that we are not alone in this journey.

To overcome the influence of fear, we must reframe our perspective on failure. Fear often arises from the fear of failure itself (which, again, stems from the fear of judgment – "What will they think of me if I fail?," "What will I think of me if I fail?," "Will failing actually make me a failure?"). However, it's vital to understand that failure is not a final outcome; It's a steppingstone on the path to success. Embracing a growth mindset allows us to view failure as an opportunity for learning, growth, and resilience. Rather than allowing fear to paralyze us, we can use it as a driving force to push through obstacles, learn from our experiences, and ultimately achieve greater success.

An empowering mindset shift involves cultivating a strong belief in our own abilities and worthiness. Fear has a tendency to undermine our self-confidence and make us doubt ourselves. By nurturing self-belief and practicing self-compassion, we can counteract these self-doubts. Recognizing and celebrating our strengths, accomplishments, and unique qualities reinforces our confidence and helps us overcome the negative influence of fear. Developing a deep sense of self-worth enables us to approach challenges with courage and resilience.

Stepping outside our comfort zones (aka enlarging the size of your comfort zones) and embracing discomfort is another fundamental aspect of this empowering mindset shift. Fear often keeps us confined within the familiar and prevents us from taking risks. However, growth and success lie just beyond the boundaries of our comfort zones. By actively seeking out challenges, embracing discomfort, and pushing ourselves beyond what is comfortable, we expand our horizons, develop new skills, and build resilience. Each time we confront a fear and emerge stronger on the other side, we gain confidence and prove to ourselves that we are capable of achieving more than we ever imagined.

Shifting our perception of judgment and criticism is crucial in overcoming fear's influence on success. Fear of judgment can inhibit us from expressing our authentic selves and pursuing our goals wholeheartedly. It's important to remember that not everyone will understand or appreciate your journey. Embracing your individuality, focusing on your own values and aspirations, and cultivating a strong sense of self allows you to move forward confidently, despite the potential for criticism. By aligning your actions with your authentic self, you attract those who resonate with your vision and purpose, fostering a supportive and nurturing environment.

Cultivating a positive and resilient mindset plays a vital role in navigating fear and overcoming its influence on your journey to success. Focusing on gratitude, practicing mindfulness, and surrounding yourself with positivity contribute to a resilient mindset. By consciously choosing to shift our focus towards the positive aspects of life, we build a foundation of strength and optimism that empowers us to confront and overcome fear. Embracing challenges as opportunities for growth, maintaining a sense of gratitude for the present moment, and seeking out uplifting and supportive relationships all contribute to our ability to thrive in the face of fear.

As you read further, I want you to think about some fearful situations you have encountered in your life and think about the results you received on the other side of breaking through those fears.

I made many discoveries when I broke through one fear a day for a year (yes, 365 days in a row of breaking through fears), but the greatest discovery was that 99% of the time when I broke through my fears I, 1) felt proud of myself for having broken through that fear or 2) the results I got on the other side of the fear were far greater than I ever imagined.

Soooo, if you will feel proud of yourself or gain a much greater results on the other side of your fears, why not break through the fears and see what happens? Do It BECAUSE You're Scared.

Make this your new mantra, "Oh, that's just fear. I'm gonna do this BECAUSE I'm scared" and see how your life changes.

CHAPTER 2

· · · · · · · · ● ● ● ● ● ● ● ● ● ● ● ● · · · · ·

Defining Your Success: Liberation from Comparison's Grip

L et's now embark on a liberating journey of defining our own success, free from the suffocating grip of comparison. We will explore the power of embracing our unique journey and breaking through the fears that arise when we measure our worth against others. Drawing inspiration from my own story and experiences, we will cover the transformative potential of defining success on our own terms.

It's all too easy to fall into the trap of comparing ourselves to others. We live in a world saturated with images of seemingly perfect lives, achievements, and successes showcased on social media and in other spheres of influence. As we scroll through feeds filled with carefully curated highlight reels, it's natural to feel a twinge of self-doubt or inadequacy. We may wonder if we are measuring up, if we are enough, and if our own accomplishments are worthy of recognition.

But here's the truth: success cannot be defined by anyone else's standards. Each of us has a unique path, with our own set of dreams, goals, and aspirations. True liberation comes when we break free from the chains of comparison and embrace our individual journey with unwavering confidence and self-belief.

In my own life, I have known the paralyzing effects of comparison all too well. From an early age, I struggled with feelings of unworthiness and a desperate need for outward validation. I constantly measured myself against others, seeking external approval and allowing the fear of falling short to dictate my actions. It was a vicious cycle that stifled my growth, robbed me of joy, and hindered my ability to define my own success.

It was only when I dared to challenge societal norms and societal expectations that I confronted my fears head-on, that I began to discover a newfound freedom. I realized that success is not a one-size-fits-all concept. It's not defined by the number of accolades, the size of our bank accounts, or the number of followers on social media. True success lies in aligning our actions with our passions, values, and personal fulfillment.

It's time to define success on our own terms. Self-reflection, understanding our unique strengths and desires, and setting goals that resonate with our authentic selves will help us define success. We will challenge the notion that success is a linear path, instead embracing the idea that It's a multifaceted and deeply personal journey.

26

Throughout this chapter, you will find practical exercises, thought-provoking questions, and guidance to help you navigate the process of defining your own success. Together, we will peel back the layers of comparison and fear, uncovering the true essence of what success means to you. By embracing your individuality, valuing your progress, and finding joy in your own achievements, you will break free from the shackles of comparison and embark on a path that leads to genuine fulfillment and happiness.

Your journey is unique, and your definition of success holds immense power. Take time to dig deep within your soul to figure out what success means to you. It's time to cast aside the weight of comparison and step into a realm where your dreams, passions, and aspirations take center stage. The journey begins now, and I am honored to accompany you as we navigate the path to defining your own success, liberated from comparison's grip.

Rediscovering Your Authenticity: Embracing Your Unique Path

We're going to embark on a transformative exploration of rediscovering our authenticity and embracing our unique path. It's a journey of breaking free from the chains of comparison and reconnecting with the essence of who we truly are. Drawing inspiration from my own story and experiences, we will tap into the power of authenticity and the profound impact it can have on defining our own success.

When we constantly compare ourselves to others, it becomes easy to lose sight of our authentic selves. We may find ourselves trying to fit into molds that were never meant for us, chasing after dreams that don't align with our true passions and values. But deep down, there is a voice within us, whispering our unique desires, urging us to embrace our individuality and forge our own path.

I recall a time when I found myself trapped in the web of comparison. I looked at the achievements of others and felt a sense of inadequacy creeping in (aka Imposter Syndrome). I questioned my own worth and whether I was on the right track. It was a disorienting and demoralizing experience that left me feeling lost and disconnected from my true self.

Through introspection and self-reflection, I began to unravel the layers of societal expectations and external influences that had clouded my judgment. I realized that true success could only be found by embracing my authenticity. It was time to shed the mask of comparison and step into the light of my own unique path.

But there was a problem. As a people-pleaser, I didn't know who I was, so it was impossible for me to be authentic. I was so worried about others liking me that I spent all of my time being who I "thought" they wanted me to be; therefore, I wasn't me. It wasn't until I worked with Liz that I started to discover who I truly am. That's when I started showing up authentically.

Rediscovering our authenticity starts with self-awareness. It requires us to dig deep, to examine our passions, values, and life experiences that have shaped us. By understanding ourselves on a profound level, we can identify the pursuits that align with our true nature. This process often involves questioning the external definitions of success that have been imposed upon us and daring to redefine success based on our own terms. That in and of itself can be a scary endeavor. Standing up for your own beliefs and bucking the system is something we aren't taught to do, so it may go against your grain. Trust me, it'll be well worth it in the end.

As we reconnect with our authentic selves, we must also learn to embrace our strengths and weaknesses. Recognizing our unique abilities and talents allows us to cultivate them, harnessing them as valuable assets on our journey. Equally important is acknowledging our limitations and embracing the growth mindset that allows us to learn, evolve, and adapt along the way.

Embracing our unique path requires courage and a willingness to step outside our comfort zones. It may involve taking risks, making unconventional choices, and veering off the well-trodden path. It's in these moments of vulnerability that we truly discover who we are and what we are capable of achieving. By embracing the unknown and challenging ourselves to explore new territories, we open ourselves up to a world of possibilities and uncharted success.

"Be brave and share your weaknesses, for in your weaknesses, others see your strengths."
~Lynda Sunshine West

Oh, my. You'll NEVER guess what just happened. I almost didn't put in the quote above. Why? Because it's MY OWN QUOTE and we are taught to never quote yourself in your own book. Well, I said to myself, "Eff that, I'm quoting myself. This is my book. I'm talking about authenticity right now, so I must show up as myself. If I leave out this quote, it's me following the "norm" of what we're taught to do. I'm not writing this book to be normal and to follow rules. I'm writing this book for someone who may need to read it in order to break through the fears that are holding them back. Okay. I will leave the quote and all of the other quotes in this book that are mine."

Even though I broke through one fear a day for an entire year, I still have fears. The difference today is that I recognize that It's fear and I Do It BECAUSE I'm Scared. By me leaving out that quote, my life wouldn't change. But by leaving out that quote, it would have been me letting my fear of judgment stop me from doing what I want to do, not what society says I need to do.

We are in a whole new world. We can write our own ticket to the journey we want to be on. I am writing my book the way I want to write my book. There are no more rules when it comes to writing your story, your message, the work that will help someone else transform their life. If you've ever thought, "I want to write a book" or someone has said, "You need to write a book," then it's time to sit down and start writing. Again, there are no rules to follow (unless you want to go through a stuffy, stodgy 20th Century book publishing house).

"You set the rules to your life." ~Lynda Sunshine West

It's important to remember that our unique path is not a destination; It's an ongoing journey of self-discovery and growth. As we navigate this path, we may encounter obstacles, setbacks, and moments of doubt. But It's through these challenges that we find the strength to persevere and remain true to ourselves. It's through embracing our authenticity that we tap into an endless reservoir of resilience, creativity, and joy.

As we embark on the journey of embracing our unique path, we must release the need for external validation and comparison. We no longer measure our worth by the achievements or milestones of others. Instead, we focus on aligning our actions with our passions, values, and personal fulfillment. We find solace in knowing that our path is our own, and that true success lies in the pursuit of our authentic desires.

Remember, authenticity and vulnerability are your greatest strengths. These are the keys to unlocking your true potential and creating a life that is aligned with your deepest desires. Embrace your unique path, and let the world witness the brilliance that shines forth when you dare to be authentically yourself.

Shifting Focus from Others to Self: Breaking Free from Comparison

Let's goooooo! When we are so busy focusing on others, it's hard to focus on ourselves and what we need to do in order to change.

When I worked for law firms, they always had the People magazine and other rag mags in the lunchroom. When we were on our lunch break, we would talk about all of the people in the magazine (and not in a nice way). I used to compare myself to others not to boost myself up, but to shoot them down. That was a learned behavior from a very early age.

When I started working with Liz, I had to unlearn what I had learned so I could learn what I needed to learn in order to become a better person, the person I am today. Once I started focusing on myself and looking for the good in me, I stopped criticizing others. I started seeing the good in people instead of searching out the bad. I came up with another quote (by the way, I came up with over 700 quotes during that year of breaking through a fear every day) that goes like this:

"See yourself through the eyes of others, for others see the real you." ~Lynda Sunshine West

---

During my journey, I have met so many incredible people who have helped me to see who I truly am. It was through their belief in me that I started believing in myself. I started adopting their beliefs and started to believe myself to be who they saw me as. This one step here is my favorite of all steps on this journey to breaking through fears. You see, when people complimented me, I would dismiss it and not believe them. But when I started to accept it to be the truth of who they saw in me, I was able to adopt it as my own belief.

Shifting our focus from others to ourselves leads to breaking free from the shackles of comparison.

Theodore Roosevelt said, "Comparison is the thief of joy." When we allow comparison to enter our minds, we tend to focus on shooting down others as well as ourselves. This is a damaging way to live. It's disempowering to not only ourselves, but to those we are comparing ourselves against. Don't get me wrong. Comparison does have its place, but not for tearing down. When comparison is used in a healthy way, it's used as a catalyst for great change and appreciation for those we are comparing ourselves to.

Comparison has a way of dimming our own light and casting shadows of self-doubt and inadequacy. I spent decades of falling into the trap of comparison, feeling the weight of external expectations and the constant need for validation. It was a path that led me away from my true self, leaving me feeling lost and disconnected.

But through reflection and inner work, I discovered the profound impact of shifting my focus from others to myself. I realized that my journey was not meant to be a mirror image of someone else's. It was my own unique story waiting to unfold. I recognized that comparing my progress, achievements, and even my struggles to those of others was a futile exercise that only served to hinder my growth.

Shifting our focus from others to ourselves begins with self-awareness. It requires us to turn inward and explore our own passions, values, and aspirations. By acknowledging our strengths, talents, and the unique experiences that have shaped us, we lay the foundation for celebrating our individuality. It's in this process of self-discovery that we begin to recognize the innate beauty and potential within ourselves, realizing that our path holds significance and purpose.

One of the most empowering steps in breaking free from comparison is practicing self-compassion. We must learn to embrace our imperfections, acknowledge our own worth, and cultivate a nurturing and supportive relationship with ourselves. By treating ourselves with kindness, understanding, and forgiveness, we create a space for growth and self-acceptance. On my own journey, I learned the importance of celebrating even the smallest victories, acknowledging my progress, and embracing the process rather than fixating on the end result.

Redirecting our focus from others to ourselves also involves setting healthy boundaries with external influences. In a world where social media and the constant barrage of information can trigger feelings of comparison, it becomes essential to curate our own reality and protect our mental well-being. It may require limiting our exposure to certain platforms or intentionally seeking out positive and uplifting content. By curating our online and offline environments, we create a supportive space that fosters self-acceptance and encourages personal growth.

In this journey of breaking free from comparison, it's important to remember that progress is not linear. We may find ourselves slipping back into the comparison trap at times, and that is perfectly normal. What matters is our commitment to redirecting our focus and nurturing a mindset of self-compassion and self-appreciation. It's a continuous practice that requires patience, perseverance, and a deep understanding of our own worth.

By shifting our focus from others to ourselves, we reclaim our power and embrace the fullness of our own journey. We learn to honor our unique path, celebrating our achievements, learning from our mistakes, and staying true to our authentic selves. In doing so, we create a life that is not defined by external comparisons but by our own personal growth and fulfillment.

Stop putting others on a pedestal and tap into your own true authentic self. Once you focus on you, you will no longer feel the need to compare yourself and you'll experience a whole different life, one filled with joy and self-fulfillment, no longer looking outward for approval because all of the approval you need is within you.

Cultivating Personal Standards: Creating Your Definition of Success

By cultivating personal standards and creating our own definition of success, we become empowered to break free from societal expectations and embrace our unique paths. Drawing inspiration from my own journey and experiences, we will uncover the power of authenticity and personal fulfillment.

Cultivating personal standards starts with a fundamental shift in perspective – it requires us to challenge the external measures of success that society imposes upon us. It's about recognizing that our journey is deeply personal and that our definition of success may differ from those around us. By letting go of comparison and societal pressures, we create space for our true desires and aspirations to emerge.

One essential step in cultivating personal standards is aligning our actions with our values. Our values serve as guiding principles that reflect what is truly important to us. By identifying and honoring these values, we establish a solid foundation for our definition of success. It's through the alignment of our actions with our values that we find a deep sense of purpose and fulfillment.

To cultivate personal standards, it's extremely important to clarify what success means to you on an individual level. Success doesn't mean the same thing for everyone. Most people use money as a barometer for success, but that's not true. Success is highly subjective and varies from person to person. Reflect on what truly brings you joy, satisfaction, and a sense of accomplishment. Consider your passions, talents, and the impact you want to make in the world. Allow yourself the freedom to create a unique definition of success that resonates with your authentic self.

Creating your definition of success also involves setting meaningful goals that reflect your values and aspirations. These goals should be driven by intrinsic motivation rather than external validation. When we pursue goals that align with our personal standards, the journey itself becomes a source of fulfillment and growth. Celebrate your progress along the way and embrace the learning experiences that come with it.

Cultivating personal standards requires courage and resilience. As you break free from societal expectations, it's highly possible that you will encounter resistance or judgment from others. Stay committed to your own path and surround yourself with a supportive network of individuals who uplift and encourage you. The people I've met on my journey have been amazingly supportive and if it wasn't for their support and belief in me, I may have gone back to my old habits (negativity and extreme sarcasm being two of them). Remember, it's your definition of success that matters, and you have the power to create a life that aligns with your deepest desires. Once you know what success means to you, you can forge ahead and become confident in standing up for your own beliefs. This one realization might be all you need in order to transform your life.

Throughout this journey, it's imperative to maintain a growth mindset, embrace challenges as opportunities for growth and learning, and see setbacks as valuable lessons that contribute to your personal development. Your personal standards will continue to evolve as you gain new insights and experiences. Embrace the flexibility and adaptability needed to refine your definition of success along the way. Your definition of success will undoubtedly change as you grow and meet new people.

The journey of cultivating personal standards is a continuous process of self-discovery and growth. Embrace the freedom and joy that come with creating your own definition of success. Trust in your innate wisdom and intuition as you navigate your unique path. You have the power to design a life that reflects your true values, passions, and aspirations. Let your personal standards guide you toward a future that is deeply fulfilling and authentically yours.

F.O.C.U.S.: Unleashing the Power of Singular Pursuit

Follow

One

Course

Until

Successful

When I first heard that phrase, I LOVED it. But then it dawned on me, I have a freakin' squirrel brain and have a hard time focusing on one thing. Plus, I'm a multi-passionate person and love doing a lot of different things at one time.

A few months ago, I was sitting at my desk and felt this pain in my chest. It was that pain that many of us experience, the pain of overwhelm. You know how it makes you out of breath and you just want to throw your hands in the air, gather up all of your papers, put them into a pile, then light a match to them and start all over from scratch? If you've never experienced that feeling, that's awesome. Unfortunately, I've experienced it many times in my life (too many to count). What was different that day, though, was that I had a huge epiphany tied to my sense of overwhelm. I exclaimed (loud and in my own head), "Oh, my God. I'm creating my own chaos." I realized that the chaos I was creating started when I was a child. When I ran away at five years old and was gone an entire week, it was to get away from the abuse and the chaos. However, when I came home riddled with fears, that chaos that I was living in would become my comfort zone.

You know how there is a quiet before a storm? That's what my chaos looks and feels like inside of my body. When things are quiet, just wait, a storm is a brewin' and it's gonna spew all over the place.

Having this awareness that I create my own chaos was huge for me. Once we have awareness, we can effect change (if we choose to).

Drawing inspiration from the philosophy of focused action and my own experiences, we will discover how harnessing our focus can lead us to extraordinary achievements and fulfillment.

In a world filled with distractions and countless opportunities, it's easy to become overwhelmed and lose sight of our goals. We often find ourselves multitasking, attempting to juggle multiple projects and responsibilities simultaneously. However, spreading our focus thin can hinder our progress and dilute our potential for success. It's in this realization that the concept of F.O.C.U.S. becomes paramount.

By embracing the principle of Follow One Course Until Successful, we are able to commit ourselves to the power of concentrated effort. We shift our attention from a scattered approach to a deliberate and focused one. Through this unwavering dedication, we tap into a reservoir of energy, clarity, and momentum that propels us forward. We become unstoppable forces, channeling our energy and resources toward a singular goal.

I have witnessed the extraordinary transformations that occur when we adopt a mindset of singular pursuit. When I shifted my focus from multiple endeavors to one core objective, I experienced exponential growth and achievement. It's through this firsthand experience that I invite you to explore the profound impact of F.O.C.U.S. on your own journey.

I started my entrepreneurial journey at age 51. Not only did I spend the first seven years figuring out who I serve, how I serve them, and how can I make money serving them, I also invested over $200,000 on products and services to help me figure it all out. By doing so, my husband and I almost became homeless because I wasn't a good steward of my money. I kept thinking, "This is it. This is the thing that will make me money while helping others." Then I failed at "the thing."

After I published my first collaboration book, *"Momentum: 13 Lessons from Action Takers Who Changed the World,"* I had had so much fun that I decided to do it again. So I created my next two collaboration books, *"The Fearless Entrepreneurs"* and *"Invisible No More; Invincible Forever More."* Again, I had a blast. But I was missing a HUGE element. I lost money on all three books. I didn't know what I was doing, but I was having fun. All three books hit #1 International Bestseller status in less than 12 hours, so I decided to do it again, but this time to focus ONLY on the book publishing.

That was my magic key.

You see, in seven years of business, the most amount of money I made in my business in any given year was $33,000. My husband and I sold my childhood home, sold 85% of our belongings, moved into a 25-foot 5th wheel trailer, and became campground hosts so I could follow my dream and passion of being a successful entrepreneur.

After seven years and doing what needed to be done in order to become successful, I finally figured it out. My eighth year in business saw a 490% growth in revenue. It was through me Following One Course Until Successful that led to that growth. Now that I know what it takes to become financially successful, it's easy.

In this chapter, my goal is to help you learn the principles of F.O.C.U.S. and how it can guide you in achieving your goals. We will explore practical strategies and techniques to help you maintain focus, overcome distractions, and stay aligned with your chosen path. We will also address common challenges and misconceptions surrounding focus. We will navigate the waters of self-doubt, resistance, and fear that often arise when we commit to following one course. By understanding these obstacles and learning to navigate through them, we can strengthen our resolve and propel ourselves toward success.

I invite you to embrace the concept of F.O.C.U.S. with an open mind and a willingness to embrace change. Are you prepared to challenge the status quo and step outside of your comfort zone? By immersing yourself in the power of singular pursuit, you have the potential to achieve remarkable results and transform your life in ways you may have never imagined.

The Art of Prioritization: Identifying Your Key Objectives

Prioritization is a crucial skill in the journey of focused action. By identifying our key objectives, we lay the foundation for successful and purposeful pursuits. Drawing inspiration from my own experiences and insights, we will explore practical strategies to help us align our priorities with our deepest aspirations and values.

Prioritization is about making conscious choices and allocating our time, energy, and resources to what truly matters to us. It's a process of discernment, where we evaluate the importance and impact of each objective in relation to our overarching goals. By prioritizing effectively, we create a roadmap that guides our actions and maximizes our productivity and fulfillment.

In my own journey of singular pursuit, I reached a pivotal moment where I realized the need to identify my key objectives. I was overwhelmed by the multitude of opportunities and responsibilities vying for my attention. It was a moment of clarity when I recognized that I couldn't do it all and that I needed to focus my efforts on the areas that aligned most closely with my passions and values.

Identifying key objectives starts with self-reflection and introspection. Take the time to examine your goals, dreams, and aspirations. What truly matters to you? What are the activities, projects, or endeavors that resonate deeply with your core values? Consider the impact you wish to make in the world and the legacy you want to leave behind. By gaining clarity on your priorities, you pave the way for focused and meaningful action.

It's essential to assess the potential impact and alignment of each objective. Not all goals are created equal, and not all endeavors will contribute equally to your vision of success. By evaluating the importance, urgency, and alignment of each objective, you can make informed decisions about where to invest your time and energy. Prioritization requires us to let go of non-essential tasks or projects that distract us from our key objectives.

One valuable approach to prioritization is my free download called, "Do It! Delegate It! or Dump It!,"[1] a simple and effective tool for

---

1 Download a free copy of Do It! Delegate It! or Dump It! at www.ActionTakersPublishing.com.

categorizing tasks based on their importance and urgency AND (for you entrepreneurs out there) the tasks that can make you money. As a business owner, without making money your business is just a hobby (which is awesome, not doesn't make for a viable business). Do It! Delegate It! or Dump It! helps to distinguish between what is truly important, what can be delegated, and what should be dumped. By focusing our efforts on tasks that are both important and aligned with our goals, we ensure that our actions have a meaningful impact.

Additionally, it's crucial to consider the resources required for each objective. Evaluate the time, energy, and skills necessary to pursue a particular goal. Be realistic about your capacity and the trade-offs involved. Prioritization requires us to make choices and sometimes say no to opportunities that don't align with our key objectives. We need to know what our key objectives are, though, in order to say no. By saying no to someone, we are actually saying yes to ourselves. It's time to own our time and say yes to what serves us and our mission. By doing so, we create space for the endeavors that truly matter and increase our chances of success.

It's important to remain flexible and adaptable because opportunities that can help propel you further faster might show up. Being rigid is a slow path to success (if ever). Embrace the dynamic nature of your journey and be open to reevaluating and readjusting your priorities accordingly. As you gain new insights and experiences and meet new people, you may discover new objectives that align more closely with your evolving vision of success.

The art of prioritizing is empowering and allows you to allocate your time and energy to what truly matters. By identifying our key objectives and aligning our actions with our deepest aspirations, we set the stage for focused and purposeful pursuits. Embrace the journey of self-discovery and prioritization, and let your key objectives guide you towards a life of fulfillment and meaningful achievements.

Laser-Like Concentration: Harnessing Focus for Optimal Results

Being laser-focused creates the ability to propel us toward optimal results and MUCH faster. Laser-like concentration is the art of directing our attention and energy toward a specific task or objective with unwavering intensity. Nothing can shake you or knock you off of your perch when you're laser-focused. Think about a lion in the jungle. You've probably seen some nature programs that show them focused on their food. Once they see the exact right opportunity, they pounce into action and the family eats that day.

When you're that focused, how much do you accomplish? What does it take for you to move into that space of focus? What are some tasks that you look at the clock and wonder, "Wow! Where did the time go?" These are likely tasks that you enjoy so much that no matter how much time has passed, you get lost.

Being laser-focused is about immersing ourselves fully in the present moment and channeling our mental and emotional resources into the task at hand. By cultivating this level of focus, we unlock our full potential and enhance our ability to achieve extraordinary results.

As I sat down to write this book, I made a declaration, "I am writing this book today." I have the skills and tools to do so. All I needed was that laser-focus to make it happen. I'm in chapter 3 and have been at it for a couple of hours.

Why did I set this goal? Because I'm speaking at an event in a few weeks and want to have my book on hand for the book signing event. If I don't finish the book, I won't have it ready for that event. Sometimes it takes an outside force to help us move into focus mode and sometimes we can tap into ourselves to get it. When we know what we need in order to get focused, we just need to do that. Yeah, yeah, it might not always be easy. I get it. But when you do encounter those focused times, cherish and make the most out of them.

I have encountered numerous distractions and obstacles that threatened to derail my progress. However, I discovered that when I harness the power of laser-like concentration, I am able to transcend these challenges and tap into a state of flow where time seems to stand still. This heightened level of focus allows me to produce exceptional work and make significant strides toward my goals.

To harness focus for optimal results, creating an environment conducive to concentration is a key to success. Minimize external distractions by eliminating unnecessary noise, turning off notifications on electronic devices, and creating a designated workspace free from clutter. Set clear boundaries and communicate your need for uninterrupted time to those around you. By cultivating a physical environment that supports focus, you create the conditions for deep concentration and productivity.

In addition to external factors, cultivate an internal state of focus. Begin by setting clear intentions and defining specific goals for each task or objective. Clarify the desired outcome and the steps required to achieve it. By having a clear roadmap, you can direct your attention and energy with precision and purpose. Do It! Delegate It! or Dump It! will help you with all of this.

One technique to enhance laser-like concentration is the practice of mindfulness. Mindfulness involves cultivating a non-judgmental awareness of the present moment. By training our minds to stay present and fully engaged with the task at hand, we reduce mental clutter and increase our capacity for sustained focus. Incorporate mindfulness techniques such as deep breathing, body scans, or meditation into your daily routine to enhance your ability to concentrate.

Recognize that maintaining focus requires mental discipline and the ability to manage internal distractions. Our minds can easily wander (there's that good 'ol squirrel brain again), leading to thoughts of self-doubt, worries, or unrelated tasks (like watching cat videos). When you notice your attention drifting, gently bring it back to the present moment and the task you are working on. Practice self-compassion and patience as you navigate the ebb and flow of concentration. Don't get mad at yourself. Just know that you are in a state of awareness that you must shift your mindset and come back to where you were. Remember that focus is a skill that can be honed through consistent practice and effort.

Another essential aspect of harnessing focus is managing our energy levels. Pay attention to your physical well-being by engaging in regular exercise, getting sufficient sleep (last night was a hard one, so I'll take a nap today), and nourishing your body with healthy food. Physical vitality provides a solid foundation for mental focus and alertness. Listen to your body's needs and prioritize self-care to optimize your ability to concentrate.

Throughout this process, it's important to remain resilient and adaptable. Recognize that distractions and unexpected challenges may arise, and setbacks are a natural part of the journey. Embrace them as learning opportunities and opportunities for growth. Reframe setbacks as feedback that can guide you toward refining your focus and enhancing your performance.

It's time to cultivate the ability to harness focus for optimal results and unlock your full potential on your path of singular pursuit. Remember, laser-like concentration is not just about getting more done; It's about immersing yourself fully in the present moment and bringing your best self to each task. By harnessing focus, you tap into a wellspring of productivity, creativity, and fulfillment. Embrace the power of laser-like concentration and witness how it propels you toward optimal results in every area of your life.

Persistence in Action: Navigating Challenges Along the Way

Persistence is a vital role in our journey of focused action. Persistent action creates results. If you give up on yourself along the way, you will not attain the success you're so badly craving. Persistence is the unwavering commitment to continue moving forward despite obstacles, setbacks, or doubts. It's the fuel that keeps us going when the initial excitement wanes and the road ahead seems arduous. By cultivating a resilient mindset and adopting effective strategies, we can overcome challenges and stay the course on our path to success.

When I broke through one fear a day for a year, as you can imagine I encountered numerous obstacles and moments of self-doubt. There were hundreds of times when it would have been easier to give in to the fear and uncertainty, but I made a conscious choice to persist. I held onto the belief that the rewards of facing my fears and pursuing my dreams far outweighed the temporary discomfort and challenges.

Persistence begins with a clear vision of what we want to achieve. By clarifying our goals and defining our purpose, we create a roadmap that guides our actions and provides a compass during difficult times. Reflect on your own goals and aspirations, and let them serve as a source of motivation and inspiration when faced with obstacles.

One powerful strategy for maintaining persistence is to break down your goals into manageable steps. Rather than focusing solely on the end result, identify the smaller milestones and actions that lead you closer to your desired outcome. Celebrate each small victory along the way by literally patting yourself on the back and saying, "Great job, Lynda Sunshine. You rock. Keep going. You got this." This will serve as a reminder of your progress and will reinforce your commitment to the journey.

When we embrace challenges as opportunities for learning and growth, it creates a growth and abundant mindset. Rather than seeing setbacks as failures, challenge yourself to see them as valuable feedback (I like to call them feedforward) and stepping stones toward success. Learn from your mistakes, adjust your approach, if necessary, and keep moving forward with renewed determination.

Surrounding yourself with a supportive network of like-minded individuals can also greatly contribute to your persistence. Seek out mentors, accountability partners, or a community of individuals who share your vision and can provide guidance and encouragement when faced with challenges. Find people who support you and lift you up, those who are positive and inspirational. Lean on their wisdom and support, and reciprocate by offering your own support to them when needed.

In moments of doubt or discouragement, tap into your inner well of resilience and self-belief. Recall your past successes and the obstacles you have already overcome. Remind yourself of the strength and resilience that resides within you, cultivate self-compassion and practice positive self-talk to counteract negative thoughts and doubts.

Persistence requires discipline and consistent effort. It's not always easy, and there may be moments when you feel tempted to give up; however, it's during these moments that your commitment to persist becomes most important. Remember that challenges are temporary, but the rewards of your persistence can last a lifetime.

Persistence is the key that unlocks the door to achievement. Will you open the door and walk through it? Embrace the challenges, stay committed to your goals, and believe in your ability to overcome any obstacle. Let persistence be your guiding light as you navigate the twists and turns on your journey of singular pursuit.

CHAPTER 4

· · · · · · ● ● ● ● ● ● ● ● ● ● ● · · · · · ·

The Burning Desire: Igniting Your Path to Greatness

"Desire is the starting point of all achievement, not a hope, not a wish, but a keen pulsating desire which transcends everything." ~Napoleon Hill

The transformative power of a burning desire and its ability to propel us towards extraordinary achievements is one that is inspired by the timeless wisdom of Napoleon Hill. The essence of this potent force that resides within each of us is waiting to be awakened and harnessed.

Hill's words beautifully capture the essence of the burning desire, an inner flame that ignites our passions, fuels our actions, and drives us to overcome any obstacle standing between us and our dreams. The burning desire is more than just a passing wish or fleeting hope; It's a deeply rooted yearning that permeates our being and fuels our pursuit of greatness. It's the intense, unwavering commitment to manifest our dreams into reality, regardless of the challenges that may arise along the way.

Throughout history, countless individuals have tapped into the power of a burning desire to accomplish extraordinary feats. From inventors and entrepreneurs to artists and leaders, their stories serve as a testament to the limitless potential that lies within each of us when we ignite the fire of our deepest desires.

What is a burning desire and what kind of remarkable impact can it have on our lives? By understanding the true essence of the burning desire and harnessing its energy, we open ourselves up to a world of endless possibilities and remarkable achievements. It's time to ignite the flame of our burning desires and unlock our true potential. The path to greatness awaits, and it begins with nurturing the burning desire within our hearts and minds.

Unleashing Your Inner Drive: Cultivating a Passionate Mindset

Passion is the fuel that ignites your burning desire and propels you towards greatness. It's the unwavering enthusiasm, excitement, and deep connection you feel towards your goals and aspirations. Cultivating a passionate mindset starts with a profound understanding of what truly lights a fire within your soul and aligns with your core values.

As Les Brown says, "You gotta be hungry!" He's referring to passion and drive. If you aren't hungry, you're much less likely to go after the goals you have because the goals aren't burning inside of you. You can "feel" passion. Being passionate about something is an exhilarating and deeply fulfilling experience. It's a feeling that radiates from within, infusing every aspect of your being with a sense of purpose, excitement, and enthusiasm. When you're passionate about something, you are driven by an intense and unwavering connection to your goals, dreams, or pursuits.

Passion ignites a fire within you, fueling your motivation, determination, and resilience. It creates a sense of deep fulfillment, joy, and satisfaction as you engage in activities or work that align with your passions. It's an inner compass that guides you towards a life that is meaningful and authentic to who you truly are.

When I became an entrepreneur in November of 2014, I had no idea what I was going to do, who I was going to serve, or how I was going to make any money. I knew only one thing: I had a drive and passion to be an entrepreneur and was going to do what I had to do in order to become successful.

After seven months, I lost all of our money putting on one event (Lemon Zest & Garlic Fest) so I told my husband that we had to 1) sell my childhood home, 2) sell 85% of our belongings, 3) buy a 28-foot 5th wheel trailer, 4) and become campground hosts at a local park so I could follow my dream and passion of being a successful entrepreneur.

Entrepreneurship isn't a straight line and it took seven years before I started paying myself from my business. And I wouldn't have it any other way. Wow! It's been a journey.

When you are passionate, time seems to fly by as you immerse yourself in your chosen endeavors. You experience a state of flow, where you are fully absorbed and engaged in the present moment. The outside world fades away, and you become completely immersed in the joy and fulfillment that your passion brings.

Passion provides a sense of purpose and direction. It gives you a clear focus and a deep drive to pursue your goals and aspirations. It compels you to push beyond your limits, take risks, and overcome obstacles with unwavering determination. Challenges become opportunities for growth, and setbacks become stepping stones toward success.

Passion brings an energy and vitality to your life that's contagious. It inspires and uplifts those around you, as they witness the depth of your commitment and the joy that radiates from you. Your passion becomes a beacon of inspiration, attracting like-minded individuals who share your enthusiasm and creating a sense of community and connection.

Being passionate about something also instills a sense of authenticity and alignment. You are living congruently with your true self, honoring your values and passions. This authenticity brings a deep sense of inner peace and fulfillment, as you are living a life that is true to who you are at the core.

While passion can involve hard work and challenges, it's marked by a sense of deep satisfaction and contentment. It fills your days with purpose and meaning, allowing you to wake up each morning with a sense of excitement and anticipation for the journey ahead.

Reflect on your personal journey and experiences. What activities, pursuits, or causes stir a sense of excitement and fulfillment within you? What brings you immense joy and a sense of purpose? By identifying these passions, you lay the foundation for unleashing your inner drive and creating a life infused with purpose and meaning.

"Don't ask yourself what the world needs. Ask yourself what makes you come alive, and go do that, because what the world needs is people who have come alive."
~Howard Thurman

Passion is not always immediately evident; it often requires exploration and self-discovery. Engage in diverse experiences, try new things, and step outside of your comfort zone. This process allows you to uncover hidden passions and gain a deeper understanding of yourself. Embrace the journey of self-exploration, knowing that It's through curiosity and openness that you will unleash your true potential.

Nurturing a passionate mindset requires a commitment to continuous growth and learning. Embrace a growth mindset, where setbacks and challenges are seen as opportunities for growth and improvement. Approach each experience with a sense of curiosity and a desire to expand your knowledge and skills. By embracing lifelong learning, you fuel your passion and open doors to new possibilities.

Surround yourself with a supportive network of individuals who share your passions and inspire you to reach new heights. Seek out mentors, role models, and like-minded peers who can provide guidance, support, and encouragement on your journey. Engage in meaningful conversations, collaborate on projects, and share your aspirations with those who uplift and challenge you. Together, you can fuel each other's passions and create a powerful community of growth and inspiration.

To maintain a passionate mindset, prioritize self-care and balance. Remember that sustainable success is built on a foundation of physical, mental, and emotional well-being. Take time for rest, relaxation, and rejuvenation. Nurture your body through exercise, nourishing food, and adequate sleep. Cultivate your mind through mindfulness practices, self-reflection, and personal development activities. Honor your emotions and seek outlets for creativity and self-expression. By taking care of yourself, you ensure that your inner drive remains vibrant and sustainable.

By embracing the journey of cultivating a passionate mindset, your life is guided toward a life that is rich with purpose, fulfillment, and extraordinary achievements. Embrace your passions, nurture your burning desire, and cultivate a mindset that propels you towards greatness. Your journey of unlocking your true potential begins now.

Determination and Commitment: Fueling the Fire Within

Determination and commitment ignite and sustain your inner drive. They both play a very important role in propelling you towards greatness and bringing your dreams to fruition. Determination is the unwavering resolve to pursue your goals and aspirations, even in the face of challenges and setbacks. It's the inner strength that keeps you going when the path gets tough. Determination stems from a deep belief in yourself and your vision, and it fuels your persistence to overcome obstacles along the way.

To cultivate determination, set clear and meaningful goals. Without clarity, it's impossible to know where you're going and how to get there. So get clear on your goals before moving forward. You gotta slow down to speed up. It's the universal law of clarity (it's not a real universal law, but it should be). Define what success means to you and establish specific objectives that align with your vision. Break down your goals into smaller, manageable steps, allowing you to track your progress and maintain a sense of momentum. When faced with difficulties, remind yourself of the purpose behind your pursuits (your WHY) and the impact they can have on your life and the lives of others. Embrace a growth mindset, viewing challenges as opportunities for learning and growth rather than as insurmountable roadblocks.

Commitment is the unwavering dedication and consistency in taking action towards your goals. John Assaraf of *The Secret* says, "You're either interested or committed." You can tell when you're committed to something because you actually do it and remain focused and disciplined, even when distractions or temptations arise. Commitment means following through on your promises and making your dreams a priority in your daily life. Commitment is the glue that holds your determination together and keeps you moving forward.

To cultivate commitment, align your actions with your values and long-term vision. Clarify what truly matters to you and make choices that reflect your priorities. Create a plan of action that outlines the steps needed to achieve your goals and hold yourself accountable to follow through. Develop self-discipline by establishing healthy habits, managing your time effectively, and staying true to your commitments. Surround yourself with a supportive network of individuals who share your drive and can provide encouragement and accountability along the way.

Both determination and commitment require resilience and a willingness to persevere in the face of adversity. There will be moments of doubt, setbacks, and unexpected challenges on your journey. However, it's during these times that your determination and commitment will shine the brightest. Embrace the discomfort and setbacks as opportunities for growth and learning. Stay focused on your long-term vision and the impact you want to make in the world. Draw strength from the belief that your dedication and perseverance will ultimately lead you to success.

Remember to celebrate your progress and acknowledge your achievements along the way (no matter how big or small). Each step forward, no matter how small, is a testament to your unwavering determination and commitment. Embrace the challenges and obstacles as opportunities to sharpen your skills and deepen your resolve. With determination and commitment as your guiding forces, you can overcome any obstacle and achieve greatness.

Harness the power of determination and commitment, and let them fuel the fire within you, propelling you towards your goals and dreams. You have the power to accomplish extraordinary things. Now go do it!

Embracing Sacrifice: How Far Are You Willing to Go?

To achieve remarkable results and make significant progress towards your goals, you must be willing to make sacrifices along the way. Sacrifice involves giving up certain comforts, conveniences, and short-term pleasures in exchange for long-term fulfillment and success. Sometimes the sacrifice is leaving a toxic environment filled with toxic people in order to welcome positivity. It can be scary to make this type of change, but the vast majority of the time the results is way better than staying in the toxicity.

Sacrifice is a conscious choice to prioritize what truly matters to you. It requires a deep understanding of your values, goals, and aspirations. When you embrace sacrifice, you acknowledge that there may be temporary discomfort or inconvenience on your path to greatness; however, the rewards and personal growth that await you make the sacrifices worthwhile.

One aspect of sacrifice is time management. To accomplish extraordinary things, you must allocate your time wisely and efficiently. This might involve saying no to certain distractions or activities that don't align with your goals. You might need to dedicate more hours to your craft, profession, or personal development. By sacrificing leisure time or less productive activities, you create space for focused effort and progress towards your goals.

Financial sacrifice is another aspect to consider. Building a successful career, launching a business, or pursuing a passion project often requires financial investment. This may involve cutting back on unnecessary expenses, budgeting diligently, and making strategic financial decisions. Sacrificing short-term luxuries can pave the way for long-term financial stability and the resources needed to support your aspirations.

Sacrifice also extends to personal relationships. Sometimes, pursuing your dreams means making difficult decisions that impact your relationships. It may involve setting boundaries, communicating your priorities, and being mindful of how your pursuits affect those closest to you. While It's important to nurture and maintain healthy relationships, it may also require letting go of toxic or unsupportive influences that hinder your progress.

Embracing sacrifice is not always easy. It requires discipline, resilience, and a clear understanding of your purpose. It's crucial to periodically reassess and reaffirm your commitment to your goals, reminding yourself of the greater purpose behind your sacrifices. Recognize that sacrifice is not about deprivation or punishment but rather a conscious investment in your personal growth and the realization of your aspirations.

While sacrifice may involve giving up certain things, it also opens up doors to new opportunities and experiences. When one door closes, many doors may be opened and you get to choose which door to walk through. It challenges you to tap into your resourcefulness, creativity, and determination. It strengthens your character, instilling resilience and perseverance in the face of challenges. By embracing sacrifice, you are actively shaping your path and creating the conditions necessary for extraordinary success.

As you navigate the terrain of sacrifice, it's important to maintain a balanced perspective. Find ways to nourish your well-being and prioritize self-care amidst your dedication to your goals. Remember that sacrifice is a means to an end, and it shouldn't overshadow your overall happiness and fulfillment.

CHAPTER 5

· · · · · · ●●●●●●●●●●●●●●● · · · ·

Wisdom Beyond Opinion:
Navigating the Realm of Counsel

In the pursuit of our dreams and aspirations, we often seek guidance and advice from others. We recognize the value of wisdom and perspective that can be gained through the counsel of others. However, not all counsel is created equal, and not all opinions hold the power to propel us toward success. I can't express enough how important It's to seek wisdom beyond mere opinion. Opinion comes from Aunt Betty, while counsel comes from someone who is <u>successfully</u> doing what you want to do.

In our journey to break through fear and achieve greatness, we encounter numerous crossroads and moments of decision-making. At these pivotal moments, the counsel we receive can have a profound impact on the direction we take and the actions we choose. It's crucial to surround ourselves with individuals who possess wisdom, experience, and a genuine interest in our growth and success.

However, not all advice is created equal. We must be discerning in choosing our mentors and confidants, ensuring that their guidance aligns with our values, goals, and aspirations. Wisdom goes beyond mere opinion, as It's rooted in knowledge, understanding, and the ability to offer insights that resonate with our unique circumstances.

In this chapter, we explore the qualities to consider when seeking counsel and the importance of nurturing relationships with mentors who can offer valuable guidance and support. We delve into the art of distinguishing constructive criticism from destructive feedback, understanding that not all opinions are conducive to our growth. By developing the skill of discernment, we empower ourselves to filter through the noise and extract the wisdom that will truly serve our journey.

Wisdom beyond opinion invites us to challenge our own beliefs and perspectives, to embrace diverse viewpoints, and to seek counsel from those who have achieved what we aspire to. It encourages us to remain open-minded and receptive to feedback while maintaining a strong sense of self and purpose.

The Power of Selective Guidance: Seeking Valuable Mentors

Selecting the right mentors who can offer valuable insights, wisdom, and support is a crucial step towards unlocking our true potential. Great mentors are individuals who have walked the path we aspire to tread AND have achieved successful results. They have faced challenges, overcome obstacles, and achieved the success we seek. Their experiences, knowledge, and perspectives provide us with a valuable roadmap as we navigate our own journey.

Not all mentors are created equal. Be selective and intentional when seeking mentorship. A great mentor isn't necessarily someone you actually get along with and can be someone who actually scares the crap out of you, but the right mentor will guide you to success. The power of selective guidance lies in finding mentors who align with your values, understand your aspirations, and genuinely care about your growth and development.

When selecting mentors, consider their expertise and experience in the specific areas you wish to excel in. Look for individuals who have achieved remarkable results and possess the skills and insights you seek to acquire. Their expertise should complement your goals, offering guidance that is relevant and applicable to your journey.

Beyond expertise, seek mentors who demonstrate qualities such as empathy, compassion, and a genuine interest in your success. Mentors who invest time in understanding your unique circumstances and challenges can provide tailored advice and support. Their guidance goes beyond generic suggestions, as they are attuned to your individual needs and aspirations.

One valuable aspect of mentorship is the ability to provide perspective. Mentors can offer insights and alternative viewpoints that challenge our limited beliefs and expand our understanding of what is possible. They can guide us in reframing our fears and help us develop the mindset necessary for growth and success.

In your search for valuable mentors, explore different avenues and networks. Look for individuals within your professional field, attend networking events, and join communities or organizations where like-minded individuals gather. Online platforms, such as mentorship programs or industry-specific forums, can also be valuable resources in connecting with mentors who can offer guidance and support.

Remember that mentorship is a two-way street. As you seek guidance from mentors, be prepared to actively engage in the relationship. Show appreciation for their time and insights, and be willing to listen, learn, and implement their advice. When you implement their advice, come back and tell them how it worked out and ask them for more advice. Simply because you implemented what they recommended, they will see that you are a great mentee. My mentor talks about how I actually do the work when he recommends something for me to do and he keeps giving me more because he knows I'll do it. Cultivate a mindset of curiosity and humility, recognizing that mentorship is a continuous learning process.

While your mentor provides valuable guidance, it's important to remember that you ultimately hold the power to shape your own journey.

Use the insights and wisdom from your mentors as a springboard for your own growth and development. Adapt their advice to fit your unique circumstances and objectives, embracing your own creativity and individuality.

By harnessing the power of selective guidance, we open ourselves up to a world of possibilities. Through the wisdom and support of valuable mentors, we can navigate the challenges, break through fear, and accelerate our journey towards success.

Discerning Advice from Noise: Differentiating Opinion from Wisdom

Because of social media and the ease of connecting with people, we often encounter a barrage of advice and opinions from various sources. Friends, family, colleagues, and even strangers may eagerly offer their perspectives on what we should do, how we should act, and the path we should take. However, opinions are just that, opinions. They may have our best interest in mind, but they don't know how to counsel us on what we're doing to help us become successful. While opinions may be plentiful, wisdom is the treasure we seek – insights that are grounded in knowledge, experience, and a deep understanding of the human journey.

You may have heard the saying that "false evidence appears real" when it comes to fear. Similarly, false wisdom can masquerade as genuine guidance. It's up to us to cultivate the discernment necessary to differentiate between the two.

When evaluating advice, consider the source. Does the person offering their opinion possess the expertise, experience, or knowledge relevant to your specific situation? Are they genuinely invested in your growth and success? Beware of well-meaning individuals who may project their own fears, limitations, or biases onto your journey. Seek counsel from those who have walked a similar path, achieved what you aspire to, and can provide insights based on firsthand experience.

Beyond the source, examine the substance of the advice. Does it align with your values, aspirations, and goals? Does it resonate with your authentic self? Sometimes, advice may be well-intentioned but not necessarily applicable to your unique circumstances. It's essential to remain true to your own vision and objectives, using the guidance you receive as a tool for growth rather than blindly following every suggestion.

Another critical factor in differentiating opinion from wisdom is understanding the underlying motivations behind the advice. Some individuals may offer advice based on their own agendas, seeking to steer you towards a particular outcome that benefits them rather than genuinely supporting your growth. Be mindful of ulterior motives and listen to your intuition when evaluating the intentions behind the guidance you receive.

The journey of discernment requires introspection and self-awareness. It necessitates developing a deep understanding of your own values, strengths, and weaknesses. By knowing yourself, you can

DO IT BECAUSE YOU'RE SCARED

better filter advice, keeping what aligns with your truth and discarding what doesn't serve your purpose.

Cultivating discernment also means embracing diverse viewpoints and being open to constructive criticism. Wisdom often emerges from healthy debates and thoughtful discussions. Engage in conversations that challenge your perspectives, inviting different opinions and insights that can broaden your understanding of the world and your own journey.

As you navigate the sea of advice, remember that you are the captain of your ship. Ultimately, the decisions and actions you take are your own responsibility. Embrace the power of discernment to evaluate the advice you receive, weighing it against your own inner compass and aspirations.

By embracing discernment, you equip yourself with a powerful tool to navigate the complex realm of advice, distinguishing between mere noise and the transformative wisdom that can shape your path to success.

Trusting Your Inner Voice: Balancing External Input with Intuition

In our journey of personal and professional growth, we encounter numerous external influences and voices that seek to shape our decisions and actions. The opinions of others, societal expectations, and the constant noise of the world can easily drown out our own inner voice. Strike a delicate balance between external input and our innate intuition.

Trusting your inner voice means developing a deep sense of self-awareness and cultivating a strong connection with your intuition. It requires honing the ability to listen to that inner whisper, that quiet guidance that comes from within. This inner voice often holds valuable insights, wisdom, and a profound understanding of your unique path.

In a world saturated with external opinions and advice, it's easy to lose touch with our intuition. We may second-guess ourselves, constantly seeking validation or approval from others before making decisions. However, true empowerment comes from recognizing that you possess an internal compass that can guide you towards your authentic path.

Trusting your inner voice creates moments of stillness and solitude in your life. In the midst of the chaos and noise, carve out time to connect with yourself. This can be through practices such as meditation, journaling, taking quiet walks in nature, and sometimes it's simply sitting in your car by yourself with no distractions. By creating space for reflection and introspection, you allow your inner voice to rise above the external clamor.

As you tune into your intuition, pay attention to the physical sensations and emotions that arise. Your body often provides subtle signals, indicating what feels right or wrong for you. These sensations may manifest as a deep sense of calm and alignment when a decision resonates with your true self, or as a subtle unease or tension when something is misaligned.

Trusting your inner voice does not mean discounting the wisdom and guidance of others. External input can be valuable and provide different perspectives that enrich your decision-making process. However, it's important to discern which advice aligns with your intuition and resonates with your authentic self.

One way to balance external input with your intuition is by seeking mentors and advisors who respect and encourage your inner voice. Surround yourself with individuals who empower you to trust your own judgment, while offering guidance and support based on their expertise and experience. A mentor who values your intuition can help you navigate the fine line between external advice and your internal compass.

As you cultivate trust in your inner voice, be prepared to make choices that may defy societal norms or expectations. Embrace the courage to follow your intuition, even when it diverges from the opinions of others. Someone I know who also publishes collaboration books informed me that "You can't fill more than one collaboration book at a time." I said, "Oh. I didn't know that. I'm filling 11 right now." That person is counsel for me in many areas, but this one area was one I didn't listen to because I was already filling those books when they said it to me. I listened to my inner voice and did what I was called to do. Remember that your path is unique, and your inner voice holds the wisdom to guide you towards your own definition of success.

· · · · · · ●●●●●●●●●●●●● · · · · · · ·

CHAPTER 6

Breaking the Chains: 7 Simple Steps to Fearless Breakthroughs

F̲ear has a way of constraining us, holding us back from reaching our full potential. It wraps around our dreams, chaining them to the realm of the impossible. But within each of us lies the power to break free from these chains, to shatter the barriers that fear has erected. In this chapter, we will embark on a transformative journey, exploring seven simple steps that can lead us to fearless breakthroughs.

Imagine a life unburdened by the weight of fear, where possibilities stretch out before us like an open road, waiting to be explored. It's within our reach, and the key lies in our willingness to take action, to confront our fears head-on, and to cultivate a mindset of empowerment.

"Nothing Happens Without Action."
~Lynda Sunshine West

These seven steps will act as your guiding light illuminating the path to fearless breakthroughs. They are not theoretical concepts, but practical tools that you can wield in your everyday life. Each step builds upon the previous one, creating a powerful synergy that propels you forward on your journey of personal and professional growth.

Throughout this chapter, we will delve deep into each step, exploring its essence, understanding its significance, and learning how to apply it in our own lives. By weaving together practical strategies and personal insights, we will forge a path that is deeply rooted in authenticity and fueled by our burning desire for growth.

As we embark on this journey, remember that breaking free from fear requires commitment, courage, and a relentless pursuit of personal evolution. It's not a linear path, but one filled with twists and turns, ups and downs, forwards and backwards and sideways, moments of triumph and moments of challenge. Yet, with each step we take, we inch closer to the freedom we seek.

So, I invite you to join me as we explore these seven steps, unlocking the potential within ourselves, and embracing the fearless breakthroughs that await us on the other side. Together, let us break the chains that bind us, and step into a future where fear no longer holds dominion. The time has come to embark on this transformative journey and claim the fearless breakthroughs that are rightfully ours.

Recognizing Fear Patterns: Identifying Your Personal Obstacles

Fear often operates in subtle and intricate ways, disguising itself in various forms and weaving its threads into the fabric of our lives. To break free from its grip, we must first recognize its patterns and identify the personal obstacles that stand in our way.

Recognizing fear patterns requires a deep level of self-awareness and introspection. There's that self-awareness thing again. It's through awareness that we can effect change. It's a process of peeling back the layers of our experiences, beliefs, and thought patterns to reveal the underlying fears that hold us back. This process may evoke vulnerability and discomfort, but it's through this courageous exploration that we can gain invaluable insights into our personal obstacles.

When you start to feel queasy in the stomach, legs shaking, throat locking up, and perspiring on your forehead, it's likely fear showing up. By tuning in to how your body is reacting to a situation can lead to you successfully breaking through that fear. When your body is feeling weird, begin by reflecting on your past experiences and patterns of behavior. Are there recurring themes or situations that evoke fear or anxiety? Notice the patterns that emerge when you face challenges or step outside of your comfort zone. Do you tend to retreat, procrastinate, or make excuses? Or perhaps you find yourself caught in a cycle of self-doubt or negative self-talk.

As you dive deeper into what you're feeling, pay attention to the underlying emotions that accompany these patterns. Fear can manifest as a range of emotions, including anxiety, doubt, insecurity, and even anger. By recognizing the emotional signals, you can start to uncover the specific fears that underlie your obstacles. When you know the underlying fear, you can change your "reactions" to the fear.

When I broke through one fear every day for a year, discovering from where/when my fears stemmed (mostly my abusive childhood) helped me to more easily break through those fears. For example, my greatest fear was the fear of judgment. I realized that was my greatest fear by listening to my body, then paying attention to where I was feeling anxious, then asking what was causing that particular fear, then discovering where it came from, then figuring out what steps I needed to take to have that fear take a back seat so I could break through it so I could gain the amazing results that were waiting on the other side of my fear.

Journaling is known to be a powerful tool in this process. Set aside dedicated time to write about your fears, experiences, and observations. Don't just write about your fears, but read what you wrote and ask yourself questions like, "What is causing this fear?," "What one step can I take right now to help me break through this fear?," or "If I do _____ [name your fear], will it adversely affect my life one year from today?" Allow your thoughts and emotions to flow freely onto the pages, without judgment or self-censorship. This practice can unveil hidden patterns, reveal deeper insights, and bring clarity to the obstacles that hinder your progress.

Additionally, seek support from trusted individuals who can offer objective perspectives. Engage in meaningful conversations with mentors, coaches, or close friends who can provide insights into your blind spots and help identify recurring patterns. Their observations and feedback can serve as valuable mirrors, enabling you to see aspects of yourself that may have been previously hidden.

It's important to remember that fear patterns and personal obstacles are unique to each individual. While certain fears may be commonly experienced, the specific triggers and underlying causes can vary greatly. Embrace the opportunity to explore your own unique journey, uncovering the intricacies of your fears and obstacles.

By recognizing fear patterns and identifying your personal obstacles, you lay the foundation for transformative growth. This self-awareness empowers you to consciously confront and address the challenges that arise, rather than allowing them to control your actions and limit your potential. It's through this process of recognition that you gain the clarity and insight needed to navigate the subsequent steps toward fearless breakthroughs.

By developing a keen awareness of your personal obstacles, you pave the way for profound transformation and open the door to a future defined by courage, resilience, and fearless breakthroughs.

Rewiring Your Mind: Strategies for Rewriting Fearful Thought Patterns

Our minds are so powerful and shape our perception of the world and influence our actions. When it comes to fear, our thoughts can either reinforce its grip or become the catalyst for liberation. What I've found interesting during my journey is that two people growing up in the same household experiencing the same exact situations can react differently. Some will excel BECAUSE of the situation and others will fail BECAUSE of the situation.

Here are some strategies for rewiring your mind and cultivating a positive, empowered mindset that transcends fearful thought patterns. When we become powerful over fear, we are empowered and can do anything we set our minds to.

Awareness and Mindfulness: The first step in rewiring your mind is to cultivate awareness of your thoughts. Pay attention to the narratives that play out in your mind when faced with fear. Are they self-limiting, negative, or based on past experiences? By becoming aware of these thought patterns, you gain the power to interrupt them and consciously redirect your focus towards more empowering thoughts.

Practice mindfulness to bring yourself into the present moment. Engage in activities such as meditation, deep breathing exercises, or mindful movement to quiet the mind and create space for new thought patterns to emerge. Mindfulness allows you to observe your thoughts without judgment, fostering a sense of detachment from fearful narratives and opening up possibilities for new perspectives. As my mom always said, "You gotta slow down to speed up."

Reframing and Positive Affirmations: Once you are aware of your fearful thought patterns, it's time to reframe them into more empowering narratives. Challenge negative self-talk by consciously replacing it with positive affirmations. For example, if a fear arises, such as the fear of failure, reframe it as an opportunity for growth and learning. Repeat phrases like, "I embrace challenges as stepping stones to success" or "I am capable of overcoming any obstacle that comes my way." When I'm in a storm (so to speak), I first become aware that I'm in the storm, then I ask God, "What am I supposed to be learning in this situation?" There is always a lesson in everything if we are open to receiving the lesson.

There's a saying, "When the student is ready, the teacher will appear." The reality is that the teacher is ALWAYS there, but the student isn't ready to see the teacher. Teachers come in the form of people or situations. We can learn from everything going on around us. Being open to the growth will help you more easily break through your fears.

Visualization and Mental Rehearsal: Utilize the power of visualization to rewire your mind and overcome fear. Imagine yourself successfully navigating through the situations that trigger fear. Visualize the desired outcomes, feeling the emotions of confidence and triumph. Engage all your senses to create a vivid mental picture of your fearless self. By repeatedly rehearsing these positive scenarios in your mind, you reinforce new neural pathways that support courageous action.

Cognitive Restructuring: Challenge and question the validity of your fearful thoughts. Are they based on objective reality or distorted perceptions? Engage in cognitive restructuring by examining the evidence for and against your fearful beliefs. Replace irrational thoughts with rational ones, emphasizing your strengths, past successes, and the potential for positive outcomes. This process allows you to reframe fear-inducing situations and approach them with a balanced and rational mindset.

Surround Yourself with Positive Influences: The people we surround ourselves with greatly impact our mindset. Seek out individuals who radiate positivity, motivation, inspiration, courage, and resilience. Engage in conversations and activities that uplift and inspire you. Their perspectives and experiences can reinforce your belief in your own abilities and provide valuable support as you work towards rewiring your mind.

When I started my personal development journey, I had no idea how pivotal hanging out with positive and uplifting people would be. I remember the day well. I was hosting an event and was standing in front of the crowd. I was about two months into breaking through one fear a day, so I had broken through 60 or so fears. Standing in front of the audience, with a little trembling in my voice, I said, "I made a life's declaration this morning. I will spend the rest of my life having as much fun as possible, hanging out with positive and uplifting people who are making a positive impact on the planet." What was weird is immediately after I said that phrase out loud, I had a tremendous amount of fear wash over me. I was scared that the people in the audience would judge me and tell me how self-centered my declaration was. On the contrary, about 20 people approached me when I was done speaking and told me that they loved my personal life's declaration so much that they wanted to adopt it.

A rewiring of my brain was taking place, but it took time, consistency and patience. It's an ongoing practice, one I practice still (several years after I broke through one fear a day for a year). Be compassionate with yourself as you navigate this process, as old thought patterns may resurface from time to time to time to time. Celebrate each small victory along the way, recognizing that every effort to shift your mindset is a step towards greater fearlessness and personal growth.

By implementing these strategies and actively rewiring your mind, you create an internal environment that nurtures courage, resilience, and self-belief. Fearful thought patterns lose their power as you cultivate a positive, empowered mindset that transcends limitations. With each rewiring, you strengthen your ability to confront fears head-on and embrace the transformative journey towards fearless breakthroughs.

Taking Bold Action: Implementing Practical Steps for Fearless Breakthroughs

Breaking through fear requires more than just introspection and mindset shifts; it demands taking bold and practical action. The 7 simple steps to break through fear every time provides a roadmap for implementing courageous actions and achieving fearless breakthroughs. Are you ready to transform your entire life? Yeah, I wasn't either, but I did it and It's the greatest thing I've ever done. It opened so many doors that I didn't even know were closed.

Step 1: Identify the Fear: The first step is to identify the specific fear that you want to overcome. Whether it's speaking on stage, asking for a raise, or starting a new venture, pinpoint the fear that holds you back from pursuing your goals and living a fulfilling life.

Step 2: Clarify the Consequences: Take a moment to reflect on the potential consequences of not confronting the fear. Visualize how your life may be impacted if you allow fear to dictate your actions. By acknowledging the negative outcomes of inaction, you create a compelling motivation to move forward.

Step 3: Evaluate the Realistic Impact: Shift your perspective and evaluate the realistic impact of confronting the fear. Consider the likelihood of the worst-case scenario actually occurring. Often, our fears are exaggerated, and the perceived risks are not as significant as they seem. Rationalize the situation and remind yourself that the potential rewards far outweigh the potential risks.

Step 4: Create a Plan: Develop a plan of action to confront the fear head-on. Break down the process into smaller, manageable steps that gradually expose you to the fear. This progressive approach allows you to build confidence and momentum as you tackle each step along the way.

Step 5: Take Immediate Action: Don't allow fear to paralyze you with indecision or delay. Take immediate action, even if It's a small step. By taking action, you demonstrate to yourself that you are capable of moving forward BECAUSE of fear's presence. Each step forward builds your courage and resilience.

Step 6: Embrace Discomfort: Understand that discomfort is a natural part of the growth process. Embrace the discomfort and recognize it as a sign that you are pushing your boundaries and expanding your comfort zone. Stepping outside of your comfort zone is where true growth happens.

Step 7: Celebrate Victories: Acknowledge and celebrate each milestone and victory along the way. Recognize the progress you have made, regardless of the outcome. Celebrating your courage and resilience reinforces a positive mindset and strengthens your belief in your ability to overcome future challenges.

By implementing this practical framework and integrating your 7 simple steps to break through fear every time, you create a structured approach for fearless breakthroughs. This framework empowers you to move beyond analysis paralysis and take decisive action towards your goals, despite the presence of fear.

Remember, each fearless breakthrough is a stepping stone on your journey of personal growth and transformation. Even if the outcome is not exactly as expected, the act of confronting fear and taking bold action opens doors to new opportunities, expands your horizons, and reinforces your inner strength.

As you navigate the path of fearless breakthroughs, be patient with yourself. Fear will still arise from time to time, but armed with this practical framework and your 7 simple steps, you possess the tools to face it head-on. With each courageous action, you become more resilient, more confident, and more adept at navigating the challenges that come your way.

Embrace the power of practical action, implement your personalized framework, and embark on a journey of fearless breakthroughs that will shape your life and propel you towards success, fulfillment, and the realization of your true potential.

Fear can either fuel you or fail you; you choose.

CONCLUSION

Congratulations! You have reached the end of this transformative journey, exploring the depths of fear and discovering the remarkable power that lies within you. Throughout this book, we have delved into the intricacies of fear, its impact on our lives, and the extraordinary potential that awaits us on the other side of it.

Remember, fear is not an enemy to be avoided or conquered; It's a companion that accompanies us on our path to growth and achievement. It's in embracing fear, acknowledging its presence, and mustering the courage to take action that we unlock our true potential and experience the exhilaration of living life to the fullest.

By breaking through the barriers of fear, you have gained invaluable insights and practical tools to navigate its grip on your success. You have discovered that fear often masks itself as self-doubt, insecurity, and the fear of judgment. But armed with self-awareness, mindset shifts, and a burning desire to transcend limitations, you have become the master of your own destiny.

Through the chapters, we explored various strategies for overcoming fear. We learned the importance of defining our own success, free from the chains of comparison. We harnessed the power of focus to channel our energy towards our key objectives. We ignited the fire of passion within us, fueled by determination and unwavering commitment. We sought wisdom beyond opinion and learned to trust our inner voice while seeking guidance from valuable mentors. We rewired our minds, replacing fearful thought patterns with empowering narratives. And, finally, we took bold action, implementing practical steps to fearlessly break through barriers and achieve our goals.

But this journey doesn't end here. It's a lifelong commitment to growth, as fear will continue to present itself in various forms throughout our lives. The key is to remember that you possess the power to face fear head-on, to embrace discomfort, and to push beyond perceived limits. Each fearless breakthrough becomes a building block for the next, propelling you forward on your path to greatness.

As you close this book, take a moment to reflect on how far you have come. Celebrate your victories, both big and small, and recognize the incredible resilience, courage, and strength you have developed. Remember that you are capable of achieving anything you set your mind to, and fear no longer holds the power to prevent you from living your life to its fullest.

Embrace fear as a catalyst for growth, a stepping stone towards your dreams, and a testament to your unwavering commitment to live life on your own terms. You possess within you the power to transform challenges into opportunities, obstacles into stepping stones, and fear into triumph.

Now is the time to go forth and embrace the world with renewed vigor, unshakable confidence, and a steadfast belief in your abilities. Embrace the mantra of "Do It BECAUSE You're Scared" as a reminder that fear is not a barrier but an invitation to push beyond your comfort zone and experience the extraordinary.

Thank you for joining me on this incredible journey. May your life be filled with fearless breakthroughs, boundless success, and the fulfillment of your wildest dreams. Now, go out and embrace your fears, for within them lies the path to your most extraordinary self.

With courage and gratitude,
Lynda Sunshine West

READER BONUS!

Dear Reader,

As a thank you for your support, Lynda Sunshine West would like to offer you a special reader bonus: a one-on-one coaching call to help you break through one fear today. During this 30-minute session, you will share one fear you want to break through and Lynda Sunshine will guide you on the steps you need to take to walk through that door of opportunity and get the result you're looking for.

This one-on-one coaching session typically **retails at $500 USD**, but as a valued reader, you are granted a one-time access at no cost to you. To claim your Fear Busting Session, simply follow this link http://fearbustersession.com and sign up today.

READER BONUS!

http://fearbustersession.com

Made in the USA
Las Vegas, NV
24 July 2023

75205680R00056